GREAT IDEAS FOR
TINY
APARTMENTS

This is a Parragon Publishing Book

Copyright © Parragon Books Ltd

Parragon Books Ltd
Queen Street House
4 Queen Street
Bath BA1 1HE, UK

Original text: Alejandro Asensio
Photography: Javier Alonso
Concept and design: Sigrid Bueno

English edition produced by: APE International, Richmond, VA
Translation from German: Heustice Whiteside for APE International, Richmond, VA

ISBN: 978-1-4075-5276-7

Printed in China

GREAT IDEAS FOR
TINY
APARTMENTS

Bath · ew York · Singapore · Hong Kong · Cologne · Delhi · Melbourne

CONTENTS

INTRODUCTION

CREATIVELY DESIGNING
TINY APARTMENTS

by Silvana Díaz

NEW CONCEPTS

Living space is expensive, and the space that is available should therefore be used as effectively and creatively as possible. But limited living space is by no means a new phenomenon of our time. After World War I, a theoretical concept of how best to address this problem was already being considered. At the CIAM (International Congress of Modern Architecture, or *Congrès Internationaux d'Architecture Moderne*) held in 1929 in Frankfurt, Germany, solutions were proposed that are still valid today. If we expand our horizons beyond the Western World and into the Far East, the traditional Japanese house with its tatami mats and low tables represents the best example of flexibility, comfort, and order. Asian pile dwellings and African huts also show us how simple fabric panels can be used in small but open spaces to create separate, private areas. In our time, increasing social, political, economic, and cultural changes lead to new models for family and life. Consequently, traditional ways of living seem to have served their purpose, and alternatives to conventional designs for living space are in greater demand than ever before. The search for original solutions demands versatility, flexibility, mobility, and above all practical creativity. The designs presented in this book are based on ideas and impressions that have been gathered at exhibitions and conventions including the *Exposition Living in Motion*, the exhibition *Design and Architecture for Flexible Living* at the Vitra Design Museum (2002), *Concreta 2003* in Portugal, and *Exposition APTM* at the *Construmat 2005* in Barcelona.

MATERIALS

Intimate living spaces require an artful arrangement of furniture. Because of limited space, the movable items, in particular, should be carefully considered and purposefully positioned. Instead of excessively expansive upholstered furniture and wall units, it is often advisable to choose pieces of more sober form, ranging from simply unostentatious to minimalist. They are functional and allow themselves to be integrated into the larger design. In this case, less is often more. The material, structure, and color of the furniture should be adapted to the specific demands of the different living areas and their functions. They can thus radiate calm and peacefulness, for example, or accentuate the desired contrasts that often determine the character of a room.

COLOR COMBINATIONS

When attempting to maximize natural illumination in an apartment, the color white is the one most often used in small spaces, because white surfaces can reflect daylight into the furthermost corners of the room. Many transparent elements, which are also translucent, are used as well, when the conditions are suitable. However, colorful accents are always placed between these in order to create the necessary contrasts, whether the goal is to separate the different living areas from each other optically, or to create an atmosphere that can evoke a certain state of mind. It is common knowledge that colors have a strong effect on the human psyche, but scientific research in this area is still not very advanced. We still rely on the color theories of Johann Wolfgang Goethe, according to which warm colors have a stimulating, cheerful, and even exciting effect, whereas cool colors are calming and soothing, but sometimes also depressing. This is formulated very generally, of course, and subjective perceptions can vary significantly between individuals. Nonetheless, experience has shown that we generally adhere to this rule intuitively, and almost no one would dispute that white conveys feelings of purity, unity, and harmony.

CEILING HEIGHT

Due to the limited area, spaces in tiny apartments should be arranged according to their function. Necessity is the mother of invention, as the saying goes, and vertical expansion is therefore the most commonly employed method of exploiting the available space. The most direct use of vertical space is the construction of a platform or an intermediate level, for example as a sleeping area or office. With such an arrangement, the space underneath remains free for daytime use. The additional space gained can also be used as a storage area or a wardrobe. Vertical extension of living space can also enable a completely new lighting arrangement. Variation in height lends itself to defining the function of different spaces, each being determined by its distance from the ceiling or the floor. By this method, the conventional arrangement is interrupted and a desirable visual unity is achieved. This intentional multifunctionality is harmonized in a spatial whole.

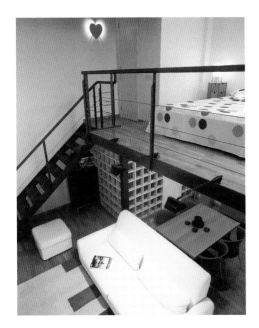

SINGULAR CHARACTERISTICS
OF THE DESIGNS

The original condition of the apartments presented in this book was in most cases poor and very much in need of renovation. They were customized to meet the demands of modern concepts of living, and their newly functional subdivision provided the basis for most of the designs. The primary goals were often to find an appropriate lighting scheme for the apartment and to achieve a visual balance between the rooms, which due to their limited width could not become too fragmented. Another priority was the creation of functional spaces, and making courtyards and terraces accessible as supplemental living areas. The materials and their uses were intended to allow the space to meld into a unified area without eliminating the apartment's original charm. On the contrary, the character already present should be given a new and better face.

The prototypes presented in this book are temporary, independent solutions that should nevertheless reflect a variety of fully realizable living possibilities. They consist of pre-fabricated functional elements that are cost-effective as well. Movable objects that can easily be stowed away, such as panels and wheeled furniture, are used most frequently. New materials and techniques are used and even borrowed from other fields— they have been designed for easy transport and easy installation.

PROTOTYPES

This book introduces prototypes of tiny apartments that were created through the collaboration of institutes, architects, and private companies. They are intended to reconcile the demand for socially acceptable living space with simultaneously low operating costs. At both the *Construmat 2005* and the *Concreta 2003* exhibitions, as well as in the case of Loft Cubes in Berlin, the following principles were established: to create rental apartments in the major cities, using very little space, with the lowest possible energy consumption and minimal construction costs. The same model applied to the most recent APTM project, which was shown at *Construmat 2005* in Barcelona. The new stipulations were to be researched in conjunction with our changing lifestyles, in order to build affordable living that meets these standards for everyone.

THE MAISONETTE

IGNACIO CARDENAL

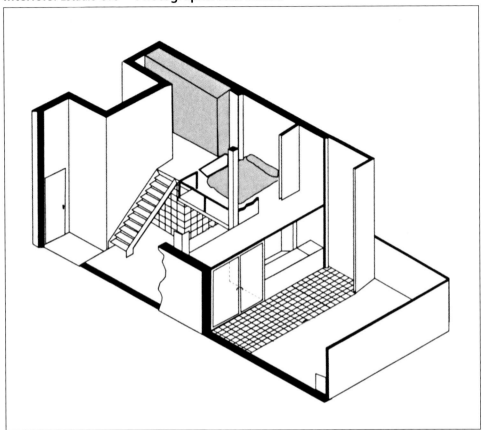

A long period of vacancy was not beneficial for this tiny apartment, but a rear courtyard that was connected to it proved to be a valuable secondary source of light. The project evolved from the planned renovation into a complete rebuilding effort, whereby the floor was lowered to accommodate the addition of a mezzanine level. For the new division of space, walls were opened up and partitions removed, thus creating greater openness. Only the bath and the dressing room are separated by doors. As the wall plaster was being removed, a brick wall was uncovered that now decoratively extends

through the whole story. The combined living and dining room is located in this area. To create an intermediate level, floor panels were inserted, and tube lights that give off a warm light were attached to the underside of these panels. The bathroom was hidden

15
THE MAISONETTE

from view with partitioning walls, and the kitchen was aligned to face the courtyard to the rear. A metal staircase connects the living area with the intermediate level, which functions as both a bedroom and a workroom. Visual continuity is achieved

17

through combining oak parquet flooring and wainscoting of the same material. The white walls modify their tone throughout the day as the exterior light falling on them changes.

19

VIBRANT RED

SERGIO STOKER

Interiors: Murray! Designagentur   **Photographs:** Javier Ortega

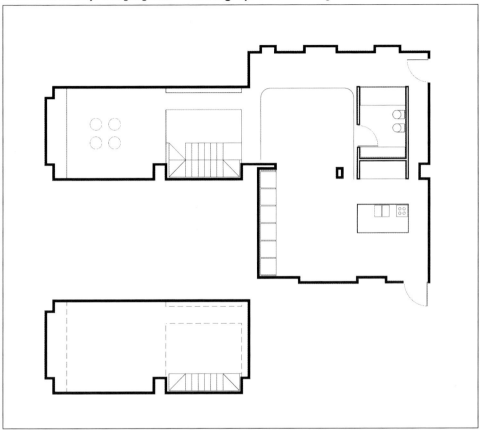

This apartment was previously an old storeroom with an area of 1100 square feet, an L-shaped layout, and a ceiling height of 10 feet, adjoined by a second level that had originally been intended as a cellar. The goals of this design were to achieve an impression of greater width and to give the individual rooms their own independent functions, in spite of the spatial and visual connectedness. The transformation of such a storeroom into an apartment required the active participation of the client and a good sense of empathetic imagination from the interior designer. The design testifies to a

preference for open space and imaginary borders that pay tribute to the apartment's industrial past. Partition walls were avoided, storage areas were concealed, and flowing space for different activities was created. On the north side of the "L" is a self-contained red block containing the bathroom as well as a kitchen island in the same color. The remainder of the ground floor serves as a living and dining room. The bedroom and dressing area are situated in the cellar. In the middle of the apartment, which opens up into three different vertical spaces, the office can be found situated between the various

levels. This interlocking of functions encourages playful experimentation with the vertical spaces and allows light to permeate to the lower level. The apartment receives daylight from the building's interior courtyard as well as from the windows facing the street. As a whole, however, the design is oriented rather to interior observation, and exhibits a minimalist division of space. The furniture and wall coverings, accordingly, were kept simple.

VIBRANT RED

CONTAINER HOUSING

GUSTAU GILI GALFETTI

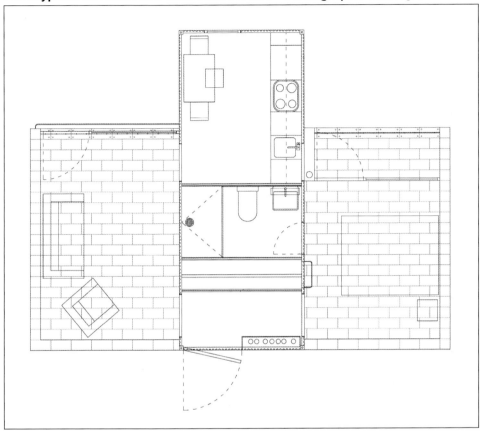

This design is conceived as a theoretical living system, rather than as a definite architectonic object. The project's realization first requires the construction of a prototype in the scale of the residential cubes. The system consists of individual units that have an area between 325 and 975 square feet, which allows great flexibility in taking into consideration the potential family situations of future residents. There is also experimentation with other combinations of the living units, for example patterns oriented toward residential blocks and towers.

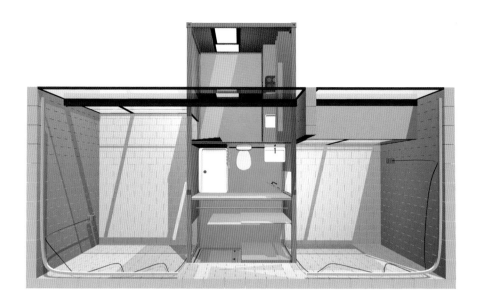

A distinction is made between two types of residential units:

a) Units that are unfinished, neutral, not further differentiated, open, and intended for their residents to complete at low cost and without great effort.

b) Units that are completely finished and equipped, compact, self-contained, and technically and industrially produced, and which have built-in bathrooms. This type automatically provides comfort and the desired living atmosphere.

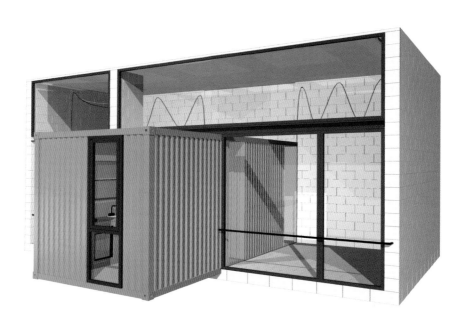

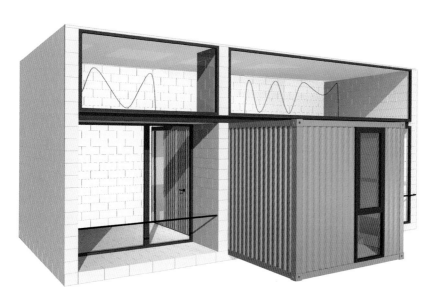

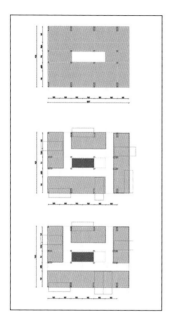

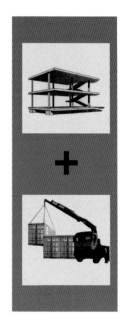

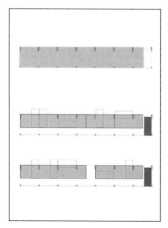

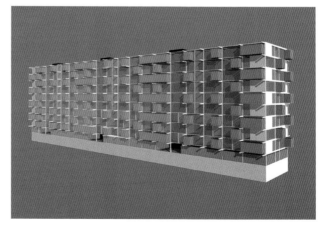

Two clearly distinct construction systems can theoretically be used for this system:

a) A free-standing structure with piles and building elements that are made of reinforced concrete for simple support surfaces, allowing optimal window area and interior furnishings, in order to insure low construction costs.

b) The construction of compact wet units in workshops through the recycling of standard containers familiar in the shipping industry, whereby surplus from the world market can be made use of, and the special characteristics of these containers (shapeable, transportable, durable, robust, exchangeable) facilitate the project.

UNDER THE ROOF

ELLEN RAPELIUS

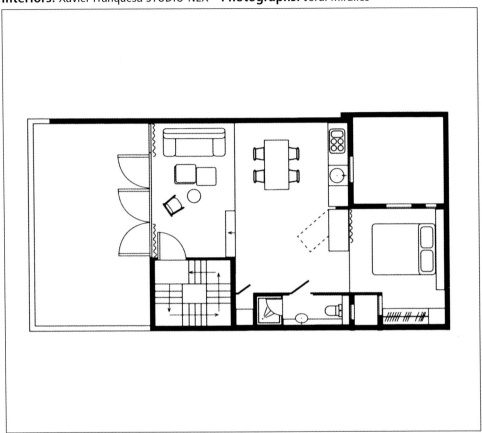

In order to customize the tiny apartment in the attic in accordance with the owner's ideas, it had to be completely renovated. Originally, the apartment was oriented toward the building's interior, away from the light and heat of the summer months. Even so, it was equipped with two balconies—one on the roof and one on the same level as the apartment itself. First, due to the limited size, all the interior walls and any obstacle to light or sight were removed, so as to provide a flowing passage from the open interior space to the balcony outside. Following the example of hotel rooms, the living/sleeping

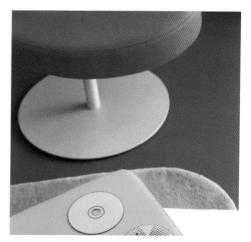

area was raised on a platform, thus separating the functions of the space without fully isolating them. Moving the kitchen and the bathroom was an essential part of the renovation. They were originally in the rear of the apartment, next to the atrium, a situation that had cut them off from the rest of the rooms.

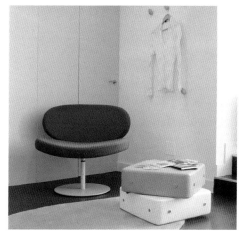

Instead, the bathroom was placed next to a ventilation shaft, and the kitchen was moved to the center of the apartment, where it is connected to the living and dining rooms. The area thus freed in the rear of the apartment became the bedroom, which is only separated from the rest of the living space by a translucent white curtain.

White dominates the atmosphere and under-scores the apartment's luminance. Pistachio green and orange furniture provide color accents. The choice of color for the Formica platform was inspired by the color scheme of the balcony and gives added emphasis to the outdoor extension of the living space.

EXPONOR HOUSE

CANNATÀ & FERNANDES

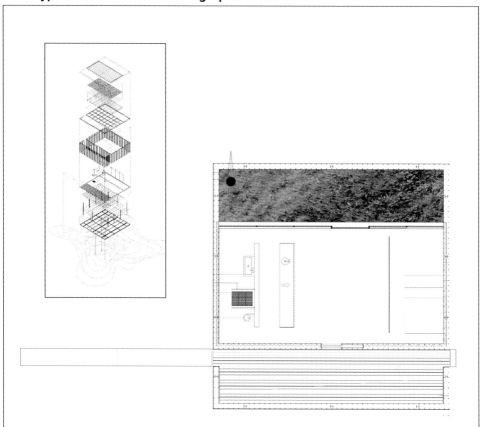

Experimentation with the improvement of the livability of houses and apartments has always been the most important of all the challenges facing an interior designer. The solution must take into account economic and technological factors as well as society's development. Unfortunately, it is usually the economic factor that puts a limit on a family's comfort. A modern family needs comfort and functionality in equal measure, but sadly, only a few of the apartments built nowadays can fulfill both requirements. Measured against what is theoretically possible in modern construction, their concepts

are enormously underdeveloped. The intention of this project's designers, therefore, is to revolutionize the building of apartments entirely. By using prefabricated building components, it is possible to achieve improved spatial flexibility, and at the same time decrease the time and effort expended. When building contemporary apartments, the following principles should be observed: the apartment must be "intelligent" and attractive, as well as functional, comfortable, logical, and economical to construct and to

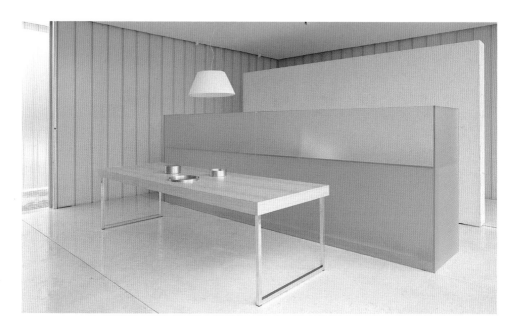

maintain. Furthermore, an apartment should provide its inhabitants with security and a protected sphere of personal privacy.

STRAIGHT LINES

ROGER BELLERA

Interiors: Produccions de Dissen y Bellera   **Photographs:** Jordi Miralles

Décor: Meritxell Moreno

This space held a great potential that was recognized and developed by the interior designers. It was a broad, open room with a high ceiling and powerful steel girders, giving it an industrial character. The designers decided to maintain this ambience. The generous vertical space allowed the addition of an intermediate level, a loft in which the bedroom was located. In the lower half of the apartment, a well-lit area for daytime activities was created. The different sections of the apartment are separated by their furnishings, but without destroying the visual unity of the space.

The color black dominates the living room, whereas the kitchen and dining area are red and white. The living room begins at the line established by the loft. The significant height of the ceiling provides much space for this area, which is conducive to the residents' communication, while the kitchen and dining area, placed as they are underneath the loft,

57
STRAIGHT LINES

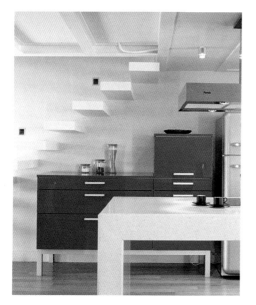

serve another function. In order to create the necessary separation of the bedroom from the more public areas, and to give the bed its own space, an L-shaped wall was built around the sleeping area. The bathroom, on the bottom floor, is reachable from the

kitchen. Directly above the bathroom, on the intermediate level, is the dressing area. A stairway without railings leads up to the bedroom. It is made of simple steps built directly into the wall and is exemplary of the elegance that characterizes the entire apartment design.

TRANSPARENCE

URBAN DESIGN

Interiors: CRU2001   **Photographs:** Albert Font   **Décor:** Mar Requena

Originally, this model was a tavern at street level: two dark floors, each with 700 square feet (65 m²), in a historical building in Barcelona's Raval district. The project was conceived with the idea that a young couple would be likely potential tenants, who would work creatively with the designers to shape this unusual space. Specialists in renovating old buildings, the team of designers decided to preserve some of the available elements, for example, the original brick walls, and to combine them with modern materials. Thus glass panels, which could serve as a visual barrier and protect privacy without cutting

off the rest of the apartment from scarce light, were introduced as partitions. For the non-translucent walls, bricks original to the building were used and combined with new plaster walls. The floor is sealed with artificial resin throughout the entire space, except in the bedrooms, in which floor coverings made of plant fibers are used. A

metal staircase, its glass railings resting on stainless steel posts, joins the different levels. By the time the renovation was complete, the space had been transformed into a versatile and well-lit apartment. What

was formerly a small bar is now equipped with two baths and two bedrooms, and offers ample living space for four people.

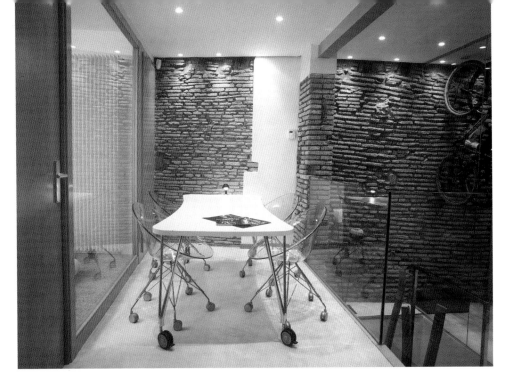

INDUSTRIAL

MUN CASADESÚS

Interiors: Arquitectura i Disseny Casadesús   **Photographs:** J. luís Hausmann

Décor: Jorge Rangel

This 540 square foot (50 m²) space was introduced at the "Exposition CasaDécor," an annual traveling exhibit of European decorative trends. This exhibition has become one of the biggest interior design shows and caters to a diverse audience with a shared interest in décor, design, and architecture. This particular project explores the potential of minimal living space and was designed exclusively for the exhibition. The result is a complex space with high ceilings and an industrial aesthetic that is especially evident in the construction elements and materials that were used for the

stairs and the other metal fittings, which are more reminiscent of scaffolding than typical residential fixtures. The loft provides open access to the living room and kitchen from anywhere in the first floor of the apartment. In a corner, fabric hung from the walls and ceiling separates the sleeping area like a theater curtain. From there, the bathroom can be reached through a glass door in the white partition wall. From the living room, a stairway leads to an intermediate level that serves as a walk-in closet, and in which the clothes hang from steel racks, as in a clothing boutique. These racks are suspended from the walls and lead along a gallery made of metal plates, whose parts again originate in construction, and which are used for the upper level. Various metal sheets, the

ceiling lights, and an abundance of stainless steel are some of the additional construction materials used. With these, the designers very consciously intended to explore the potential of industrial design for residential interiors.

79
INDUSTRIAL

CHICKEN

SANTIAGO CIRUJEDA

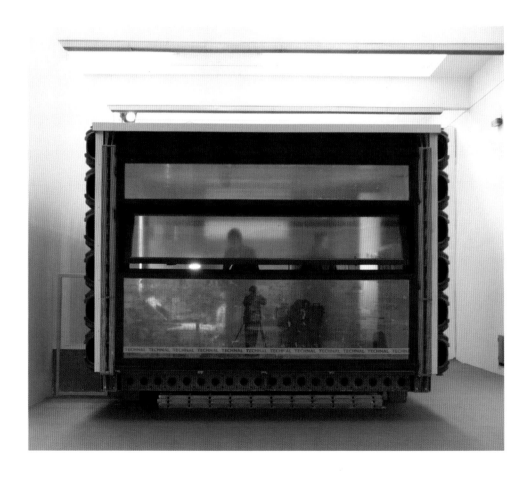

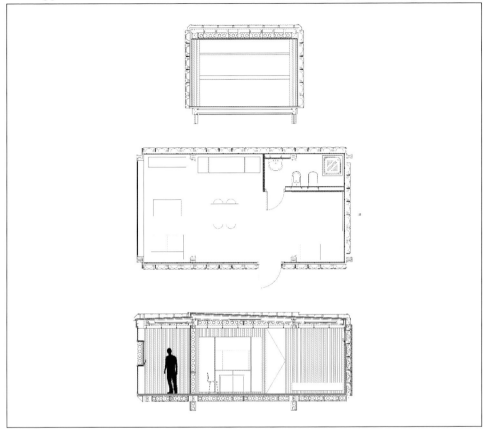

For the past several years, Santiago Cirujeda has been involved with projects that originate in urban situations, but has done so without orienting himself to conventional urbanism. Here he presents a model for mobile architecture in the Poble Sec district of Barcelona. The purpose of the project is to improve relationships between the different institutions that influence city planning. By using the APTM Exhibition to investigate new spatial dimensions in housing complexes, Cirujeda focused on the reorganization of a construction site in Barcelona. The complex was supposed to become a

85
CHICKEN

center for cultural activities that principally occur independently of each other, but that simultaneously provide opportunities for people to come together, to exchange views, and to collaborate with one another. Cirujeda is convinced that these mobile housing units could contribute to a revival of a number of neighborhoods in Barcelona's historic old city—and thus in the historic

centers of other large cities as well. With this "urban nomadism," underutilized sites can be used productively for a certain period of time. It is, in principle, the recycling of building space through the use of transferable housing modules. In order for the construction costs to pay off, changes of location should occur at intervals of no less than two years.

IN THE CORNER

SUSANA ITARTE

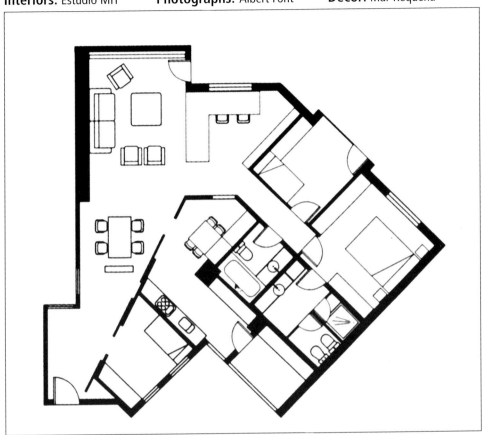

Although this apartment was very well oriented and flooded with sunlight, it was in terrible condition and the division of space was entirely unsatisfactory, consisting of small, fragmented rooms connected by exceedingly long hallways. In addition, the angular situation of the corner apartment made it very difficult to devise a sensible floor plan. The solution was the introduction of a connecting element in the middle of the apartment: a wall with sliding doors that makes the most of the generous sunlight and shortens the hallways. From the perspective of the hall in the public area of the apart-

ment, the new room distribution appears as a sequence—hall, dining room, living room, and office—that is connected both visually and acoustically. Nevertheless, the intimacy of the individual rooms is protected from the gaze of unexpected company.

95
IN THE CORNER

LIVING SPACE

JORGE CORTÉS, SERGIO GARCÍA & BORJA GARCÍA

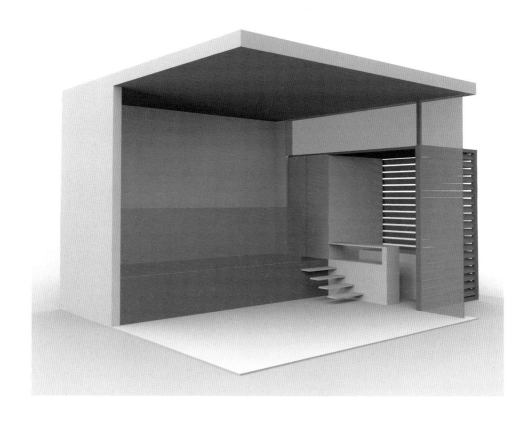

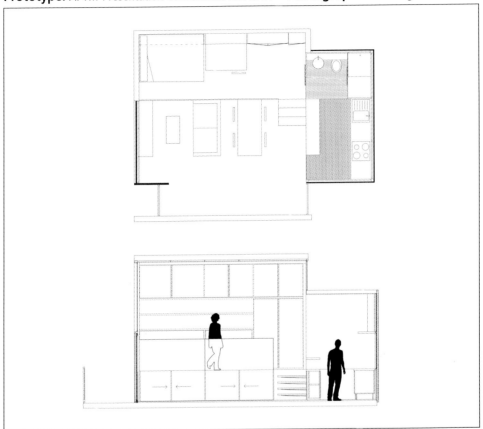

The basic idea behind this project was to utilize the available space as efficiently as possible. The apartment's different levels should be connected to their appropriate functions. In the bathroom, a low ceiling allows a broad distribution of light in the kitchen as well. The sleeping area, in the uppermost main room, was visually separated by raising the floor by two and a half feet (80 cm). The area underneath provides significant storage space that can accommodate all the furniture in the main room, if necessary. This scheme is repeated upstairs: the bed or the table can disappear,

and the bedroom becomes free space. The intimacy of the wet unit within the apartment is ensured by wooden paneling that is open, yet still maintains privacy. The basic furniture is included in cost of the apartment, whether it is for sale or for rent. In addition, the living room can be rearranged horizontally or vertically to address different needs. More precisely, there are a variety of possible configurations that combine the concept of minimal occupation of space with other concepts, such as visual expansiveness,

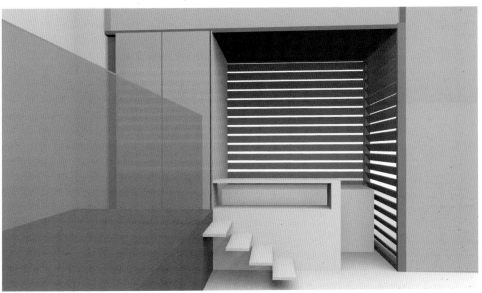

optimal utilization of space, and living quality. In short, this is a tiny apartment with an enormous quality of life. The use of prefabricated building elements, allowing quick assembly, improves efficiency and saves energy. The same is true for the apartment's interior lighting, since it is only one room, and the exterior walls have generous openings. The circulation of air made possible by these openings provides a perfect interior climate without the need for any further technology. The connectivity between the apartments is created on a

vertical level by stairways and elevators, and horizontally by corridors leading to the various living spaces, which are separated from each other optically. The spaces lying in between serve as places for residents to meet and communicate. They can also be transformed into storage space, for example for bicycles.

IN A SKIING AREA

IÑAKI FERNÁNDEZ BIURRUN

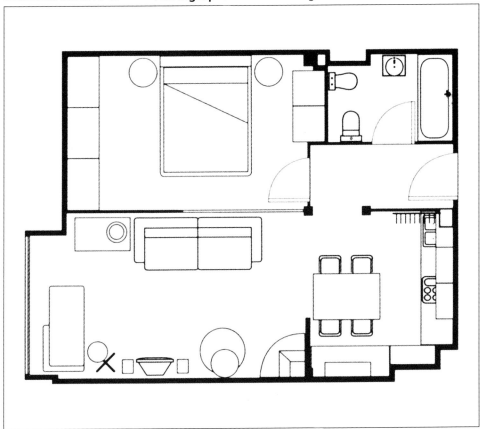

The owner of the apartment and initiator of this project was looking for housing as close as possible to the ski lifts when he found this 430 square foot (40 m²) apartment in Formigal, Spain. One window looked out onto the ski run, and another had been set into the slope of the roof. The majority of the apartment lay in darkness but offered great potential for change. The project involved renovation of the apartment's interior. First, the plaster ceiling was removed from the kitchen, hallway, and bathroom, which made it necessary to relay the water pipes and electrical system. This resulted in a ceiling

height of 13 feet (4 m), which allowed the addition of an intermediate level. Supported by fir beams, it can be reached by a staircase of wooden steps on a metal framework with railings. The staircase could only occupy a minimal amount of space, and its arrangement in relation to the kitchen cabinets was accomplished through painstakingly precise work.

Through the inclusion of two skylight windows, one of which was already in place, the upper room is now especially well lit. The separation of the bedroom from the living room and the dining and cooking areas was achieved with a partition wall, the upper border of which is made of glass. Light that penetrates the windows in the roof is thus

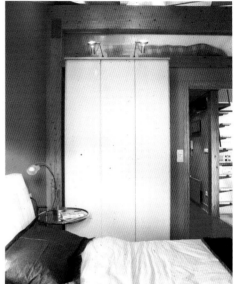

able to reach the living room. The living area is visually separated from the kitchen and dining area by a waist-high brick wall. Through the choice of color for the walls and the use of many wooden accents, a warm and comfortable atmosphere was achieved in this tiny apartment.

ROOF BEAMS

M. MARTEEN

Photographs: J. luís Hausmann   **Décor:** Jorge Rangel

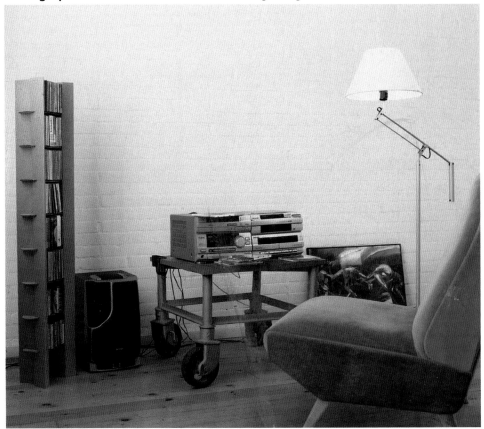

The purpose of this design was to make a rundown building in an old industrial district of Barcelona inhabitable again. Under the auspices of what is called a "22@" project, this district is being reintegrated into the fabric of the city and thoroughly modernized. Environmentally hazardous heavy industry should in time be replaced by business ventures in the areas of computer and communications technology. The space had an interesting structure to work with: it featured metal supports connecting the wooden struts of a gable roof, which was in turn carried by massive wooden beams. The

expansive ceiling height lent itself to the creation of a design that would show off this interesting system of struts. Two levels were built, distinguished by their functions. The daytime area in the lower level contains a foyer, the kitchen, the dining room, and the living room. A metal stairway with solid wood steps leads to the upper level, where the bedroom and bathroom are located. Both were housed in room modules that resemble two large, white cubes.

117

The front sides of both are open and thus connected with the living and dining rooms, and the view of the roof beams is always unobstructed. The balustrade is only as high as a low handrail, but it provides enough safety for the upper level. This also serves to reinforce the connectedness of the two levels. The stairway is located in the middle of the apartment, between the two "room cubes." This design makes use of the white

119

color of the cubes, setting up a playful contrast with the use of a clear violet for the apartment's original walls. The floor is made of wood, as are the steps and the original roof beams, which received extensive treatment to increase their stability.

SINGLE OCCUPANCY

MIGUEL ÁNGEL LLÁCER

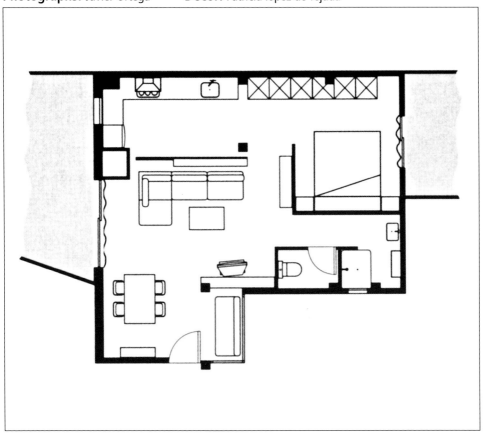

This apartment features an area of 625 square feet (58 m²). A family had lived in it previously, and it was divided into many very small rooms, an arrangement that seriously hindered natural lighting. The architect conducted a thorough renovation of the apartment, creating a space in which the different areas and functions overlap. In addition, all the separating walls were removed, one of the bedrooms was eliminated, and an original balcony was integrated into the living area. The result was a living space with only a single door—leading to the toilet. The subdivision of the living area was

accomplished with integrated partitions in a geometrical arrangement, but these do not obstruct a view of the apartment in its entirety. In this way, the sleeping area could be made an independt space, and the dining room could be separated from the kitchen.

The choice of wall and floor coverings similarly aimed to achieve a visual unity that would showcase the sleek lines and homogeneous effect of the apartment. The floor surface is the same everywhere—even in the bathroom—and the side walls as well as the

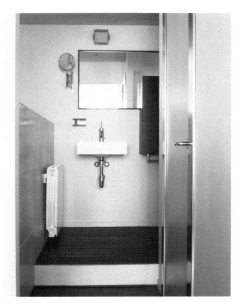

ceiling are a soft gray. The furnishings are made of stained beech wood, the only exception being the built-in closet, with its yellow lacquered doors. It fills the space between the kitchen and bedroom.

129

FACTORY

MARIA VIVES & LLUÍS ESCARMÍS

Interiors: GCA ARQUITECTES ASSOCIATS   **Photographs:** Jordi Miralles

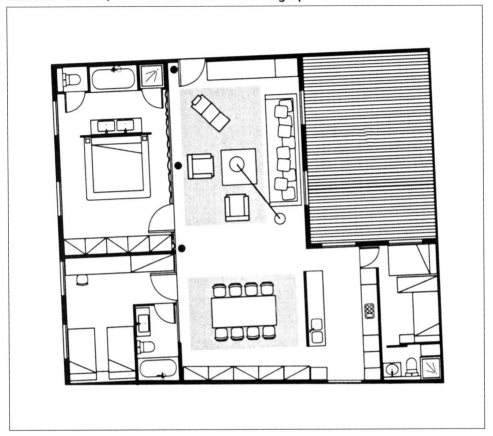

The goal of this renovation was to remain true to the space's industrial past, to maintain or even emphasize the original structure, and at the same time to provide the comfortable living space desired by the owners. The space is an almost square hall with an area of 1350 square feet (126 m²).

It features large windows, a 250-square-foot (23 m²) outdoor terrace, and a ceiling height of 10 feet (3 m). The greatest problem was caused by the wooden beams and metal supports throughout the space, as well as the bricks, vaulting, and columns that were to be preserved, but which had to be fit into

three bedrooms. The solution for the living area was as follows: the center of the space is reserved for the living room. The three bedrooms are located on the somewhat longer sides, each with its own bath. Glass plates, mounted in iron frames that have

been painted black, separate the bedrooms from each other and from the living room. Large oak panels, serving as partition walls, provide independence for the centrally located kitchen and separate the bedrooms from the bathrooms. Above one of the

bedrooms, an intermediate level was added to house a study from which the entire apartment can be surveyed. The floor, covered with large sheets of particleboard, again recalls the apartment's industrial past. The walls of the living room and the bed-

rooms were treated with a combination of brickwork and white paint. The majority of the furniture was designed by the interior designer. Otherwise, a classical yet decidedly contemporary design was favored.

INTELLIGENCE

JOAN LAO

Interiors: JOAN LAO   **Photographs:** Albert Font   **Décor:** Producciones D7

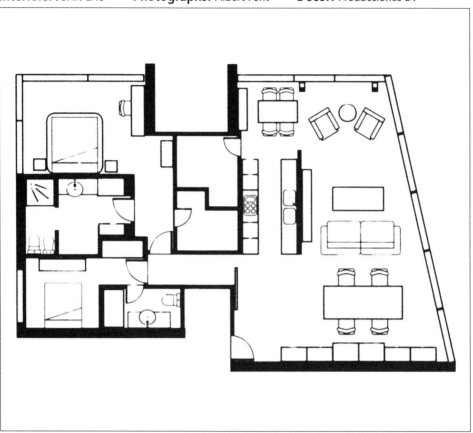

This design follows the guidelines of the apartment's owners, who wanted to integrate technology into their daily lives and are drawn to open, dynamic spaces that can be transformed as needed with little effort. The architect made use of technology that fulfills these wishes with little more than the push of a button: a central computer determines, for example, if someone is entering the apartment, or if there is a gas leak. Flowers are watered and clothes washed by remote control, and the living room can be converted into a home theater, in which a curtain serves as the screen.

The living room forms the epicenter of the apartment. The dining room and study intersect here as well, depending on how the furniture—most of which is mounted on wheels—is arranged. The only exceptions are the desk and bookshelves, which subtly conceal the cables of the technical installation. By means of built-in screens, the entire apartment can be monitored. The

overpowering natural light that floods the apartment is softened with blinds. The nocturnal illumination of the house can likewise be controlled with the central computer. As a contrast to all the technology, a natural material dominates the furnishings: warm, comfortable wood.

CENTRAL LOCATION

ARTHUR DE MATTOS

Interiors: ARTHUR DE MATTOS **Photographs:** J. Luís Hausmann

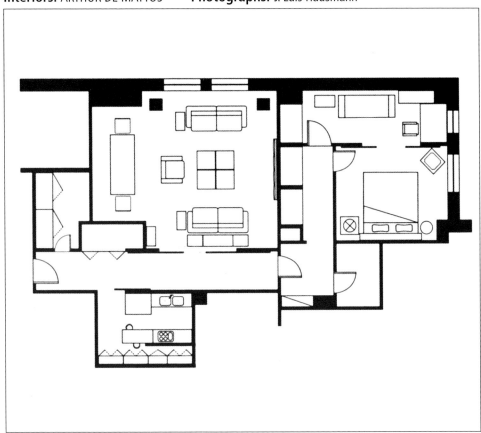

Décor: Jorge Rangel

Brazilian interior designer De Mattos comes to New York regularly on business. The location of this apartment in trendy SohHo, its eleven-and-a-half foot (3-m) tall ceilings, its renovation potential, and its southern exposure—which promised considerable brightness—were the decisive factors in the designer's choice to set up an outpost here in the "Big Apple." The 860 square foot (80 m²) studio consists of a broad, open parlor with a dining room, a bedroom with walk-in closet, a bathroom, a kitchen and a study. The parlor and dining room are the focal point of the apartment.

From these, the bedroom is reached by a corridor, thus ensuring privacy. De Mattos designed a significant portion of the furnishings in Brazil, for example the handmade rug and the square objet d'art in the parlor. The warm colors used, in combination with wood and natural fibers, convey the peaceful feeling of a retreat from the chaos of the big city.

152

INSPIRATION

CARLOS GAGO

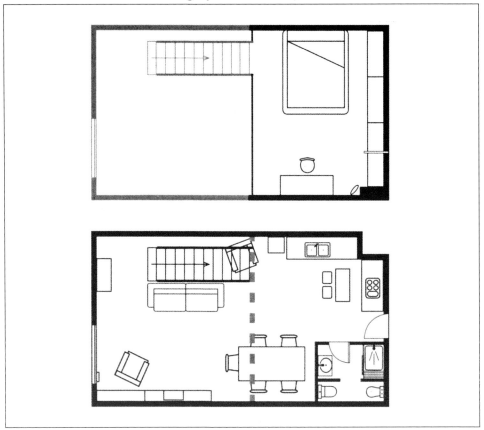

This space was originally a loft dating from the "golden age" of industrial-residential conversion. It is twenty feet wide, forty feet long, and the ceilings are sixteen feet high (6 x 12 x 5 m), thus allowing the insertion of an intermediate level that increased the floor space. One difficulty arose from the fact that there is only one window facing the street to serve as a source of daylight. Furthermore, due to the window's considerable height, it could only be reached by a ladder that had been built by the owner especially for that purpose. The intermediate level was therefore situated above the kitchen, bathroom,

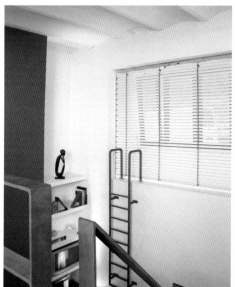

and dining room, which are in turn located opposite the window. The space immediately in front of the window was left completely unobstructed to preserve the view of the ceiling vault. The renovation resulted in two open levels. Only the kitchen and the bathroom are visually separate. In order to keep the open character of the space intact, the partition walls do not extend all the way to the ceiling or to the floor. Only where necessary—that is, in the bath, is the room

completely closed. On the lower level, the living room opens into the kitchen and the dining room, an arrangement that renders this area visible from every part of the apartment. The kitchen has an industrial aesthetic that pays tribute to the building's past. The bathroom, across from the kitchen, is built with light materials and glass. Most of the furniture is red, but it encompasses various decorative styles. It is intended to convey strength and happiness. A narrow

162

black metal staircase leads to the intermediate level, where the bedroom and wardrobe are located. Their design is based on that of the lower level: a wooden floor, white walls with red accents, and black steel beams. This room only contains a few pieces of furniture so that the observer's view is not distracted from the complex spatial structure of the room.

NATURAL LIGHT

PETER RICHTERS

Interiors: ANTONIO DE JUAN   **Photographs:** Jordi Miralles

This tiny apartment consists of one rectangular room with three openings to the side. The space was divided into a living room, a kitchen and dining area, and a bedroom. This separation into different functional areas is achieved simply through the arrangement of the furniture, since there are no walls or doors. The kitchen furniture in the middle of the room therefore functions as a sort of hub around which the structure of the rest of the apartment flows. Free space between the cabinets allows access to the bedroom, and the dining table divides the kitchen from the living room. On the long sides of the

rectangle are the bedroom and living room. They are equipped with large windows that extend from one end of the apartment to the other and fill the entire space with light. When sunlight shines through the pale curtains, it produces a gentle hue that is consistent with the apartment's furnishings. The choice of color in the kitchen, on the other hand, contrasts dramatically with the rest of the apartment: the ceiling and parts

of the décor are black. The curtains can dampen incoming light in this area if it is too intense. In order to create a similar contrast, black furniture was chosen for the bedroom and the living room, whereas the light-colored fixtures in the kitchen contrast well with the dark background.

LOFT CUBE

WERNER AISSLINGER

This project originated in two main objectives. The first was to create a minimalist, transitional apartment, and secondly, it should be able to be situated on top of the flat-roofed architecture of Berlin, thus turning the unused space on the rooftops of the metropolis into viable residential quarters.

The execution is reminiscent of experimental hippie colonies such as "Drop City" in Colorado (1965) and 1968 San Francisco, where the geodesic domes inspired by Buckminster Fuller were all the rage. The aim of the "Loft Cube" project was to create living units that could be either purchased or

rented. Thanks to a precise calculation of its weight, a crane or helicopter should be able to move an entire apartment without difficulty. In order to make the roof surfaces habitable, of course, the property rights and easements would have to be clarified. The weight of the cube cannot exceed the roof's load-bearing capacity, and each unit must

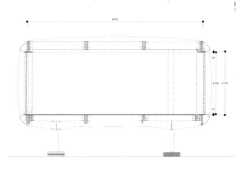

furthermore be able to resist the increased impact of the wind. The interior has a surface area of approximately 430 square feet (40 m^2) and is framed by four slightly curved panels. The resident is able to select the colors, materials, and wind resistance. The amount of sunlight entering the apartment is controlled to taste with the use of opaque or

transparent elements. A coverable skylight can also be used in adjusting light levels. The interior space is structured with partitions that slide on rails, thus creating a variable division of space determined by the arrangement of the furniture.

STUDIO WAXTER

JAMES SLADE

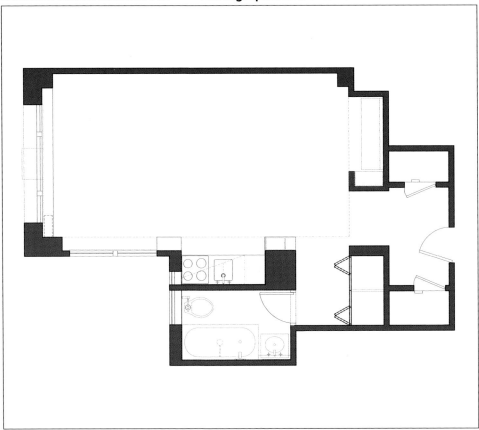

The interior designer was hired by an art dealer to reconfigure his compact apartment in a simple yet elegant manner. Flexibly defined areas that can fulfill different functions were arranged for an appropriate division of space. The apartment was intended to give the impression of one large space, as opposed to an agglomeration of distinct rooms. The apartment was furnished as sparingly as possible, and unostentatious colors dominate the decorative scheme. The kitchen recedes into a niche, and the bed can be folded into a closet when necessary, thus creating more free space.

In order to preserve the spatial unity, the walls, floors, and all the surfaces in the kitchen were painted a bright gray. The intent was to produce a neutral background for the furnishings and especially the diverse works of art. The kitchen is arranged precisely to the client's specifications.

In order to make it possible to use the very narrow kitchen window, the cabinets were mounted at an angle and fitted with glass doors, which reflect the sunlight like a mirror into the living room. Mirrors can be found in other locations as well, where they underscore the impression of spatial expansiveness. Every element in the apartment

187
STUDIO WAXTER

was carefully selected for a specific position. The former doors, except the one leading into the bathroom, were converted into tall, open portals. Curtains partially divide the individual sections and their functions from each other.

189

CONTRASTS

BENN HAITSMA

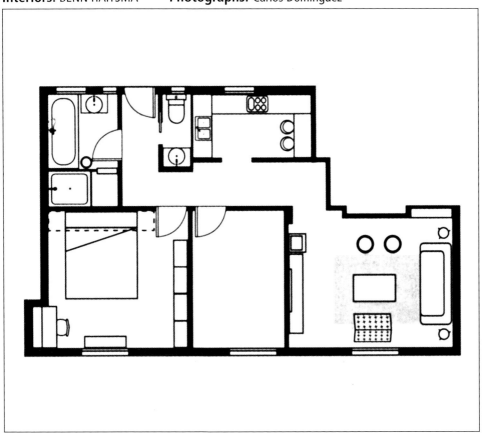

This space was originally a small, dark, and poorly divided apartment, which nevertheless had a certain appeal. After the complete renovation, only the walls of the original apartment remained. The kitchen and bathroom were entirely remodeled, and only the front door and the door to the bedroom remained intact. First and foremost, the tiny apartment had to be made brighter. The Australian origins of the owners and instigators of the project influenced the choice of color. To counteract the wet and cold London winters, they selected a palette of warm tones. The floor in the living room was

covered with dark oak from California, which contrasts effectively with the bright, cream-colored walls and ceiling. The furniture, with its differing styles, were intended to prevent an all-too-homogeneous interior. The spatial constraints nevertheless demanded that the

CONTRASTS

decorative scheme be kept rather simple otherwise. Overall, the constellation of the interior spaces achieved a playful combination of contrasting colors, stylistic currents, and varied materials.

MODULES
CANNATÀ & FERNANDES

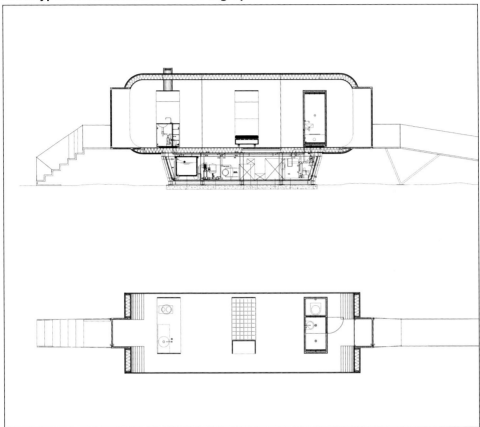

These prototypes were exhibited for the first time at CONCRETA 2003. The modules consist of combinable but individual elements that could perhaps serve as a transitional apartment, an observation room, a bar, or even as a small storage unit. The special nature of the modules lies in their functionality and versatility. They can be placed together as a building complex, or they can stand alone. In addition, they are produced with energy-saving materials, for example the roof, which contains solar cells. They are especially intended for areas in which drastic changes in the surrounding environment are

not possible or not desirable, for example research stations in nature preserves, on beaches, or in public squares. Every module is 10 by 30 feet (3 x 9 m) and has an area of 300 square feet (27 m²). The design model is

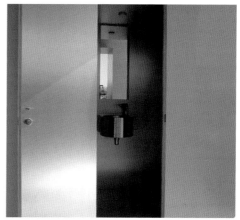

intended to consist of a single prefabricated unit. Modules are therefore not built on site, but are rather transported in one piece by truck or helicopter. This makes it possible for each module not only to be adjusted to fit

into its new surroundings, but also to be equipped in advance with environmentally sound technologies and new types of materials.

FORMER OFFICE

NEREA ETXEBARRÍA

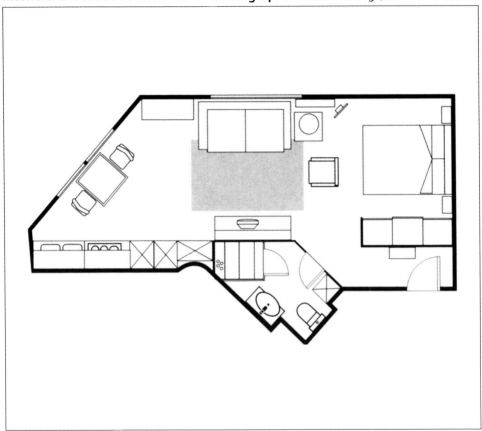

This project involved the complete renovation of a former office on a middle story. The point of departure for the design was a very large window in the facade that flooded the entire space with light. Due to the apartment's small dimensions, a division of space was not attempted, but rather the visual unity was used to full advantage. The only exceptions are a walk-in closet and the bathroom—a container of sorts, where a trapezoidal floor plan corresponds to the original geometry of the apartment. The wall separating the bathroom from the remaining space is made of slate and extends through

to the kitchen, where the accoutrements are of the same material. In spite of the limited space, the apartment contains all the typical electrical appliances, as well as an environmentally friendly and energy-efficient air conditioning system. The absence of any sort of woodwork in the apartment is noteworthy. The walls are painted a matte white

and merge into the slate floor without baseboards. Thoughtful placement of the mounted halogen lamps emphasizes the ceiling height. The room's illumination is optimized by the adjustment of each source of light to the apartment's angles.

PILOT APARTMENT

ÁBALOS & HERREROS

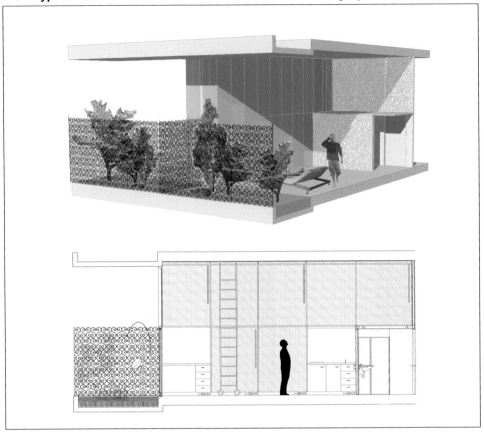

The unique quality of this design lies in an exceptional integrated wall that simultaneously serves as storage space for furniture, thus allowing the entire living room to be emptied, if necessary. The design also boasts a winter garden of sorts, with a Mediterranean ambience. The apartment is intended to be part of a complex with sixteen to twenty stories that is built of concrete slabs and is laid out in spokes around a hub. Crowning the building is an awning, under which a communal garden area can be found. Thus, natural light also reaches the common areas (entrance, laundry room,

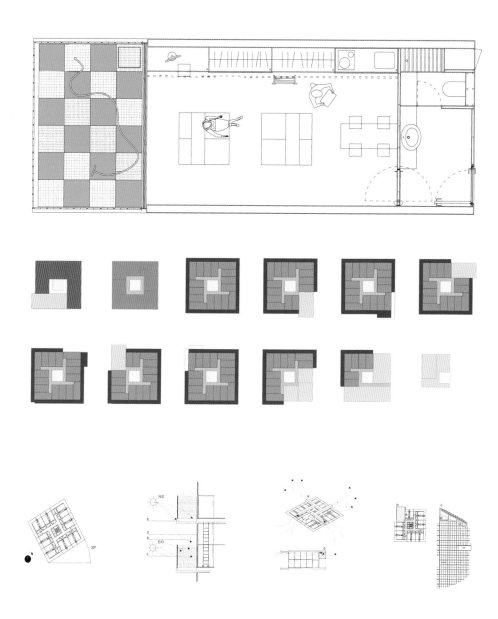

216
PILOT APARTMENT

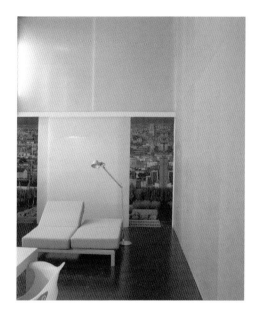

fitness room, recreation room). The building's interiors are kept exceptionally simple. The walls and ceilings are concrete slabs. There is little furniture, and tapestries cover the concrete walls. The floor is also very modest, painted a single shade of white. The individual apartments and other rooms are reached by way of corridors that meet at the center of the building, and also lead to the garden. These corridors are connected to a natural ventilation system that—thanks to the building's height—provides a pleasant atmosphere in the interior spaces.

BLACK & WHITE

JOSÉ LUIS SAINZ

Localization: ZIAKO INTERIORISMO   **Photographs:** Susana Arechaga and Luís M. Ambrós

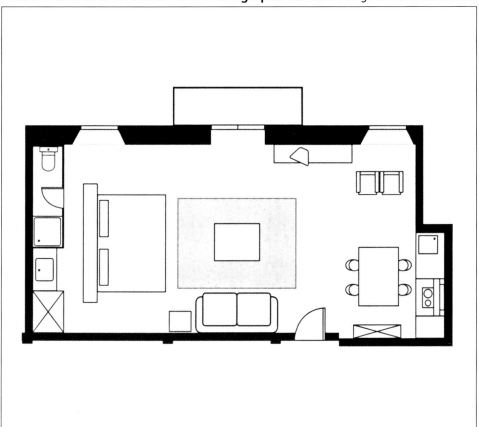

This 430 square foot (40 m²) attic apartment is in the architect's private residence. The aim of the project was to achieve unity and consistent lighting in this small area. The lack of an existing floor plan presented no problem. Since it was intended for only one person, the living space could remain completely open to view. Functionality and illumination are the key concepts in its execution. Kitchen, living room, bedroom, and bath make up one unit—an impression reinforced by the uniform choice of color. Only the bathroom and storage area have doors, which are made of textured glass.

Behind the mirror above the bathroom sink is a small cabinet for storage. The striking interplay of black and white dominates the entire atmosphere and is only interrupted by a few spots of color provided by furniture, artwork on the walls, and decorative objects.

As the architect explains, "The white flows over the walls, floors, baseboards, and ceilings, while as contrast, black was chosen for the furniture designed in our studio and the paneling." The project ultimately led to the complete remodeling of this tiny

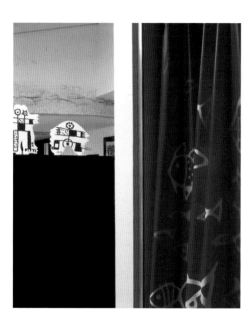 

apartment and its décor. Only the oak beams that run through the ceiling remained in their original state; they were stained white.

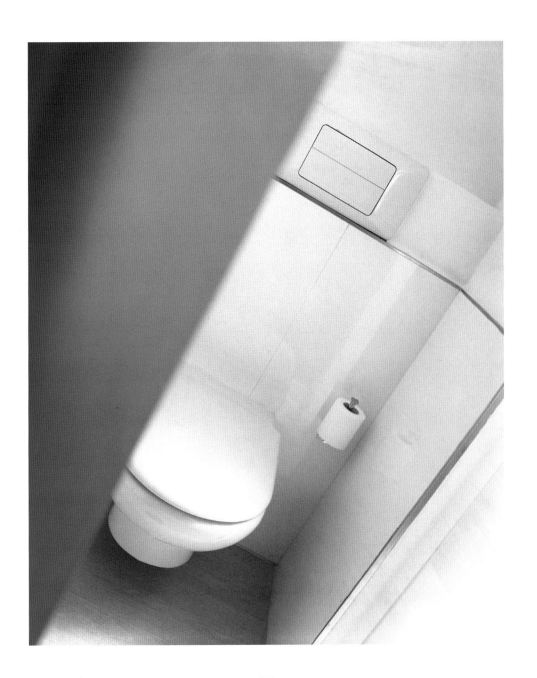

GAINING HEIGHT

CECILIA ISTÚRIZ

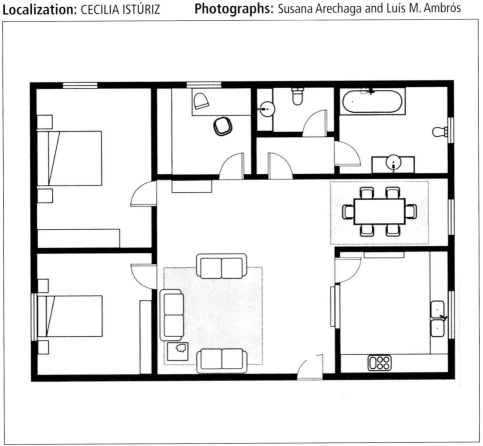

The unusual supporting-beam construction that was revealed when a ceiling was removed played a decisive role in the renovation of this free-standing, ground-floor apartment. Located in the historic old town of Hendaya, a Spanish resort, it is part of a building dating from the beginning of the twentieth century. The apartment has a slate roof as well as very high ceilings with lots of interesting angles and an exceptionally attractive vault structure. The basic idea underlying this project was to maintain and emphasize that structure. This was accomplished by keeping the central area of the

apartment and the ceiling visible, as the architect explains. Two windows were installed in the roof to provide more light for the living room in the center of the apartment, and the interior was painted white. Providing contrast, the built-in elements are painted a gentle gray, and the old oak parquet floor was restored. All the other rooms are connected by way of the living room. The dining room is attached in L-form to the living room. From here, one can reach the exterior through a door. All the remaining rooms surround this living-dining area,

as does the kitchen, which is separated by a waist-high wall with a built-in glass window. The bedroom and bathroom together form a more private unit and are both reached through separate doors. The decorator insisted on the pleasure of designing some of the furniture herself, for which she also made use of old materials. The large table that stands in the middle of the living room and the reupholstered pieces, for example, are her creations.